AF222094

My deepest thanks to

Chris(tian), Silke, Noel and Sascha

I
remain
...blind

by
Robert Grant

Bibliographische Information der Deutschen
Nationalbibliothek:
Die Deutsche Nationalbibliothek
verzeichnet diese Publikation in der
Deutschen Nationalbibliographie;
detaillierte bibliographische Daten sind im
Internet über http://www.dnb.de abrufbar.

Herstellung und Verlag:
BoD - Books on Demand, Norderstedt

ISBN 9783753490298

Contents

"They'll end up doing the same thing baby...
we'll do something different"
Conversation with Ruby, Berlin 2021

Fame =

As a younger man and for many
years, I thought I'd made it.
Was guru...the master.
Put my films and words in front of
herds of people, tending results.

As an older man,
I saw the truth of things.
That *if* I really had made it,
people would seek me out
not the other way around.

Clarified moments
amidst an industry of lies,
showed me how to be humble.
For dreamt success is facile,
it's the journey...that holds pride.

Those Days

Of warm days like these.
When summer dressed women float
on bikes through parks. As ripped
sporty types parade in sand traps,
glistening with volleyballs.

Of stoners sitting, chatting, giggling.
When families play throwing games
with hoops made of string. Clowns,
juggling whilst precariously walking
across lengths of rope with spring.

Of these days when everything seems
normal. Yet, families have to check
the floor for broken bottles before laying
out rugs. When dog shit is scraped from
athletes feet onto vandalised benches.

Of Police wailing whistles, breaking up
drunk teens holding immature beers.
When no one is really as happy as they
are now portraying. Whilst Mummy takes
a phone call...just too important to ignore.

Of couples eyeing other peoples lovers.
Photos of genitals floating through
social media offices, giving weekend
workers laughs in stuffy boxes on the
other side of the world.

Of days like these I fear for our future,
when this is what we consider as fun. All
sitting around in parks pretending to enjoy
each other's company, while really only
considering, what others look like naked.

Packaged

On similar holidays. Drinking and eating
fried things, watching the same terrible
hotel cabaret, hoping tonight will be
better than nights previous.

Watching children play basketball with
hotel mascots, dressed as cuddly tigers
in thirty degree heat…remembering
shitty jobs you did whilst in youth.

Looking down, to see an ant crawl across
this book of empty stories. Swallowing,
as I squash it with a cheap plastic flip flop,
hoping someone may do the same for me.

Some other me, with an even larger ego,
cracking me on the head. As this holiday
seams to repeat last year's calamari, with
the same hangovers and worse cabaret.

In light

We *are* the things we hold so dear,
the muffled things we cry.
Of limbo nights, after crazy days
with friends that bicker and fight.

We *are* a beautiful rhyming thing
a retrospectively ending strain.
Cast into a world that is unknown
and will never be seen the same.

Spend *our* time living up to a standard,
waved on by a gloomy foe.
Ending all and this, with smile,
sweet bliss…white tag upon your toe.

Stencils

What is to come of us now?
When life has given you enough
and all that's left is decay.
No more childish dreams, only
the reality and broken fantasies
that I have weaved so neatly
into this web of satisfaction
harbouring self depravation.

I have, everything a man could
consider that he might ever want.
Amidst illusions, tall tales and
moments of truthful friendship.
Have witnessed creation,
laughed at unfunny jokes,
recited poetry to strangers
in drunken bars. Shouted, when
shouting seams rested in silence.

This place I now find myself, seams
glad of my presence. Willing me to
entertain self confessed chess champions

looking for psychologists. Irruptions made
of fluff and other states of personality.
Whilst smiling and ordering shots with no
money in my pocket, only plastic to do
these pinpricked nights of addiction.

So there's only one thing left to come for
me now. The last eternal silence stretching
to the ends of nowhere, in no time at all.
Arching bent backs to straighten, in this
place known to me from a millennia
before my conception and will thusly
extend before me as if valid or real. I am
the memories you will read about now.

Of this game we all play and as that bell is
rung in our ears as we see the world a
very dark space, of which to fall into. We
must conceive that we are no more than
a tiny thing…no more than something so
inconsequential that we will simply tip
into infinity, holding our hands before us
to break the fall that isn't even happening.

These patterns are but parts of us, as we
are part of them. Cutting out stencils, to be

repeated of coming conversation in future drinking holes, when men that look and act exactly like me, will say that same things to other humans, who look like you or your mother. Their shadow confirming that something feels familiar about all this.

So what is to come of me now is pointless, as pointless as you reading this and coming up with conclusions that have already been made for you by me and others likewise. You can only grow your fern, repeat the pattern, for you are the only reason to see things in any other way than what has already been before, over time, over now.

Therefore you should sell the world, sell your soul, trade everything into a better version of the things you don't need or see. Eon upon millennia, fighting within an atom, handed to you for comprehension. We are finite, we are dirt, we are pollen, gliding to an outcome that is thankfully unseen, muted by swollen lips.

Trust in yourself to know nothing as you
glide through chaos, confusing compassion
with greed. For, when that day comes and
you're left to discover the answer to life's
only question. Sitting with pounding
hammers, silenced skies never seen upon
conversations never had, you'll feel how
pointless questions really seam.

Slipping into a new world, same one as
before your conception, in those eons
you don't remember, in the place that no
one ever dreams. We are the glint in the
eyes of history, as we dance our childish
parade. If you can hold your hands up and
fully admit you never have or ever will have,
any form of control.

Then happiness is yours forever.

Intoxicating

Stood one night, cooking.
I think about my daughters future.
What kind of person have I produced?
How will her world be formed?

Casually wandering over
to kitchens mouth, I find her spinning,
getting high and dizzy whilst twisting,
to a ball, on the floor.

Only to get up and repeat
the movement time and again.
Collapsing in blissful glee and
wild chuckle...with each rotation.

"Having fun baby?" I ask, sipping
red wine. Promptly returning
to the kitchen, to stir pasta and
think about Bathos, poetically.

Way

A man stands before a tattered door.

Screaming until his lungs burst.

Angry that,
        although his voice can pass through,

                his body never will.

Wine Lolly Pop

When I drink wine
my tongue goes redder
than when my daughter
sucks on cheap lolly pops.

To this day, I don't know
which one is more
destructive, Or has more
lasting physical effects.

Mouse

Without comprehension,
we are but blind moments
stumbling towards expressions
of something we never understood.
Awaiting someone to remind us,
that we didn't have a clue
in the first place.

Inbred

Alcohol solves every superficial
problem. The darker
are left to experience or
expensive therapy sessions.

Solitude being the only
answer we misunderstand.
Screaming then twisting
life on its head.

Feel the *you* come down
from the high back fences.
Finding problems to be
chased away, not burrowed.

Take solace that you know
as much as you do. Then
pick up your weapon
and go out to play.

Cat

Art enriches people
that feel personal content.
Improves life's possibilities,
yet destroys artists.

For, giving meaning to
a world draped in plastic,
enveloping so completely,
you must loose inhibition.

Chaos is true pain and in
order to make others worlds
more beautifully bearable,
you must first, bleed.

Not consider or think upon,
but dampen your hands
in buckets of sweat, poured
before crippled feet.

Give yourself over to those who
share your eyes. For they
will keep secrets between
our world and theirs.

Turn your head to tilt.
Tare the fabric straight
from its comfy sarcophagus,
leaving it nakedly bemused.

Pain to smile, emotion to song.
Lost to loved, depressed to
reasons. Loud to quiet,
confidence abundant.

Exploiting our world in
order to make you think.
As we plot elaborate ways
to take up your time.

bum rush

This pen is finally working again,
this brain, roughly the same.

Coming back to me writing
the same thing again and
again and again

                    ...these already used words,
from many points in my past,
lead eloquently hamstrung conclusions,
to rest upon miscommunication.

                    Returning briefly,

to bum rush my ego.

Damp

He sits, a day post.
Pats sanity, a damp
dog, on some morning
jumping in dark rain puddles.
So dirty as to blacken his snout,
proceeding to wash his hands
of the whole experience,
playing fetch in
the aftermath.

Beast

It's no cure to hide, you're not that good
an actor...better to know your beast,
tickle her under the chin. Control those
wicked ways that trouble you so.

If your beast be male, then I'm not an
authority. For mine is a buck toothed
bitch with a jagged laugh, ready to slice.
Taking the pain in her unique way.

She knows the secret that your body
tries to hide behind torn knuckles.
That drag on the ground, halting
evolutions in the tracks on her arm.

She sees you looking at me and knows
not to give me over. For she protects
my blind spot that you've never licked.
Knows how to throw you off guard.

She'll cut and beat you, for she's my
little beast and always was. Ready to
defend a master that can never see
her coming, yet loves her warn tentacles.

Not a word

Every choice you
think you have,
is no more than
an ink blot on a page.

Only connected
by the shape of
the letters you
eventually form.

Appreciating that
they don't or ever will
exist in nowhere like
this particular here.

Gives freedom to think
you have some form of
control over up or down.
Then quickly waving it away.

Fighting the Cold

As we played, the rain
hit hard and wet.
Lashing shop fronts
as if angry at them.
Cascading flows
bringing people to dance,
dodging droplets
like drive by bullets.

My daughter cupping her
hands under torrent guttering,
filling...freshly chilled.
As I move to halt the madness
she arches her back and
throws *acquired mischief*
directly into a shatter cold,
oncoming, face.

A chorus of laughter aided
by grandmother bystander,
mocking Daddy for not seeing
the obvious coming.
Slapped for a second,

locked in attack position,
wondering if anger or
playfulness will burst forth.

Crouching lower for better
leverage, I feel my hips
bounce with anticipation.
I need a good venting to
rid this vacuous tension,
bulging my eyes as I jolt
forward and grab that
tiny trouble maker.

I'll show her who's boss,
how dare she do that to daddy!
Swiftly wrenching her up
in explosive arms, I take
her roughly by the shoulder
and leg. Grasping so tightly,
that her silence understands
the seriousness.

Flinging through damp air,
towards an overflow pipe
I water board the
chuckling little scoundrel.

She squirms, then begins
laughing…wrestling a better
escape position, just like
I taught her yesterday.

With one twist she's free,
jumping back, mocking me, then
lunging for raindrops that
converge to solid stream.
Those crazy dog eyes,
I so love to see, mix her madness
and excitement as she and me,
play happily in a spiralling frenzy.

That old lady from before
smiles even wider now. As
this rainy interlude, on yet
another boring shopping trip,
culminates in something that
we will remember at times
in the future, when Daddy
just can't do it anymore.

But we were happy then,
now happily reminiscing.
As your hair flew through the air,

feet following suit.
We were her and me,
just us so free, helping
old ladies to experience
her own kids one more time.

Now let it rain,
so we may dance again.
Swing, kiss and laugh again.
As from there…things just got
better and better. You grew up,
I grew old but still eagerly told
these stories of children being
swung through wailing storms.

A strong wind

The people I care most about are in
the next room with hot water bottles
on their bellies.

Complaining constantly about trapped
wind, excreting air furiously, ending in
a chuckle-n-gasp.

I sit, a contented man, never happier
to hear people farting, stopping occasionally
to cackle-n-chirp.

Worth

Never tell *all* your secrets.
Save something disgraceful
for personal pleasure.

Something terribly dirty
as to solidify disgust
in your soul.

Hard Truth

This pen before me,
like five thumbs
grasping at bad
metaphors, hanging in
the air like shit stains
on yesterdays underpants.

Splendora

I turn off some random internet clip,
sit waiting for the deafening sound
of steel praying mantises shifting
concrete and glass.

Followed by a multitude of cars.
Loud Russian builders screaming to
those insect drivers, fragmenting
the eye line, of this sexy city.

Drunk teenagers add to the cacophony.
Their voices busting through floor
to ceiling windows in my expensive
mid town apartment.

Warm pink eye lashes flutter over
expensive hotel facades as day
become warm night and comforting
wink turns to promise.

What to do with time…read philosophy?
Write poetry? Drink a decent red,
write lies into stories, smile wide

and full and damp.
For I am exactly where I want to
be, in the time I want to live.
Exactly at the middle of this life
I hold so luckily.

Now let the night take me,
wink softly at the game. As this dance
within a dream that I am fully living,
can really only be mine.

Spiders

There are a
family of spiders
living in one corner
of my office.
The youngest
turns to me,
asking if I wouldn't
mind keeping it
down a bit,
as they're trying
to sleep and
can't do so, until
I stop talking
to myself.
I soon realise
that maybe twists
are not at all
valid in the art
of writing poetry
...as isn't red
wine and weed,
or so it would seem.

Never times three

My teeth itch.
Skin crawls over my back.

Unkempt moustache hairs curl
into scared nostrils.

On this morning I promised myself
it was the last time…again.

This Part

In this place I find myself
in this time I have made my own,
this slot of existence,
coin held to forehead.

If all I have to show at
the end of my life is this.
After all the wishing is done
and even more time has passed.

All that's left are these clichés
badly rumbled onto a page.
If this be times great waste,
then at least it made me smile.

Statement

I am a poet!

Nothing more or less than that.

For in of itself, is beauty enough.

THE Ruby WRITER

My daughter is standing
in front of my desk
watching me work.

Asks me if she can
use my pen, "What should
I write papa?" she asks.

Looks sideways on seeing
my fountain pen. Choosing
couch and pencil instead.

Sits for ten minutes or so
thinking about the world
and how she views it.

Mimicking every movement,
even coughing out a twenty pack
smoked whilst writing last night.

Then, simply applying one word
to the clean white page, before
placing it under my nose.

Just her name with a question
mark languish before us, as
we smile and think on the answer.

"It'll take a long time my love"
I say, as we get summoned
to the kitchen for dinner.

Stopping half way down the hallway
for a smile, whilst she draws love hearts
upon my ashen hand.

Content with the smell of mashed
potatoes...with a side of swearing,
as mummy burns the sausages...

                ...as I, question again.

Morning After

"Why are your eyes so bloodshot daddy?"

For a second I'm amazed with the
quality of her English, then am hit
with the internal discomfort of
having to answer the question.

"Daddy went out last night, sweet heart"

The best answer is always the truth,
even if two minutes does pass as
I wait to see if honesty is the best...
"Did you have fun?" it breathes, I exhale.

"Yes, daddy had a good night and yours?"

"Good" her cringed smile turns to childish
acknowledgement. Exactly as my memory
progresses to having to make breakfast,
on this trembling morning after.

"Just toast this morning my love...Ok?"

Pages Long

I spend my days doing what most
people do in their free time.
No pressure is exerted on me,
bar that to which I place upon myself.

With time for movies, music, poetry,
contemplation, regret. With families
to catch up with over stupid conversations
about decisions already been made.

This 'Foie gras' of pop culture,
neck squeezed, ingesting pointless
answers to questions that have never
been considered. These are our times.

You work your ass off, as I ponder and
write, take post lunch walks on sunny days
or pre walk naps on rainy. And even if you
think I'm wasting my time, I still sit here...

...In my underpants, writing this directly to
you with some obscure French Sci-fi film

playing in the background, on this pointless
Friday morning…technically working.
Right now, after all, you're reading
this…aren't you? Even if I'm not really
saying anything that hasn't been already
said, in these free flow times…like now.

Even though you can't really let go, even
when cooked for and cleaned after…looked
after. With wild sexual foot rubs, upon beds
that you didn't actually buy…for yourself.

Even then this is hard,
                    so I'll stop and save
                        your embarrassment.

Broke by wife

"I'm trying to be a better person, sweet.
It's going to take some adjustment"
I said one morning, amidst a gravelled
conversation over breakfast.

"It's never easy to stop doing something
you love even if you know that thing isn't
doing you any favours" her eyes now fixed
on the breadbox behind my head.

"There are substances that are put here to
help, or obscure our vision enough to fully
see the reality of now" her posture now
formed of nodding and eye brow raises.

"And some are left to report these things
they see, in a world left up to
interpretation" my arrogance explodes
as she drops her shoulders in exhale.

"I think you should go and write
that down" she says, with a smirk,
as I quickly realise that she had the
upper hand this whole damn time.

Hot?

"Warm enough is it?"
she asks rubbing sweat
from the back of her
damp, plump calves.

As the bar swells.
I sit attempting
to separate my
underpants from my leg.

"What star sign are you?"
she continues as I consider
how best to separate myself from
the rest of this conversation.

In my bar

1.

I sit chatting to a musician friend,
on my first time bar this year.
An older man, with wild white hair
sits kindly pointing my way.

I acknowledge with head bob, returning
to my friend to form conversation.
After a few minutes I stand to play
pool, passing the gentleman as I do so.

He takes my arm, stops my stride,
gleefully smiling at me educing
a head twist and curiously questioning
look. For I don't know him...do I?

"bought your book" he says
as I'm relieved I hadn't previously
annoyed him and didn't remember
what we talked about.

In the briefest of conversations,
he expresses his opinion and tells

what moved and stood him fast.
Laugh and cry and angry swell did make.

"I'm going to rejoin my friends, thanks
for your support it means everything"
I say strolling on, glancing back and realise
the old man sat at the bar is me...

        as I am him.

    ...later the same night
      at that very same bar.

2.

Drinking with a conversationalist
who's explaining one thing or another.
My drunken state not allowing me to
listen fully, yet it's interesting enough
fodder, bar chatter. When (from over my
left shoulder) I hear the slightest whisper of
something in direction towards verse. I turn
to find a middle aged man
reading poetry in my ear. This goes on for
10 minutes or so until the conversationalist
on my right has had enough and get's in a
argument about the fact that he doesn't

think *I* want to hear poetry in a bar whilst
drunk. 'I'd rather average poetry than
your nonsense rhetoric' I think
returning sharply to my drink, to
question if I should keep coming
to a bar I love so warmly…

                                        …and then

3.

I find myself here, this time,
amongst twenty some-thinks,
as regulars pass to the stalls
discussing keys and straws.

"What's your favourite book?" I ask,
in lieu of familiarity, their eyes
filled with beer and possibilities,
their skin glowing as mine once did.

He replies with the name of some book
about dragons or wizards or a
space ship commander as my head
bobs down to my beer.

I'm not sure if to comment that at
his age my jewel was '1984' by Orwell,
or even if I told him, that he would
entirely get the reference.

Not sure if either is valid or what
conclusions can be drawn from
the story, if it's even meant
to be the simple point…at all.

That point drowned in a thousand
other stories, all as pointless as
the last annoying story I listened to
whilst sat here drunk.

But maybe just that's it's point.

                                        …now sleep.

Drip

Sweat on keyboard,
drips out furious pen
upon days when hard
writing is required.
Yet astonished that
the vigorous artist
sweating may be
that it's 34 degrees today
rather than any form
of real passion.

Troop

I saw a guy,
stood at the
Brandenburg Gate
in Berlin
dressed as
a Star Wars
storm trooper.
He's either
some idiot
extracting Euros
out of
tourists...or
a satirical
genius, who
fully grasps
the base
route of
comedy and
can execute
with gusto.
Either way
the amount
of money

he's taking
proves fully
that it doesn't
really matter.
And in
this time
and in this
place he
maybe the
genius I
hope,
amongst
people
who don't
really care
either way.

Swelter

The heating
in my apartment
is so effective that
after 10 minutes
I had to open
the windows to
let heat out.
Which hardly seems like
something to write
or complain about.

The Rambling Man (redux)

For when I observe them
considering me foolish,
I see victory in their conclusion.

Left open to these interpretations,
scratching their head
as the test comes back positive.

So long as they don't get too close
I'll let them stress that they have me made,
positioned in history as that guy last night.

He who told them a story that they no
longer believe, in some badly lit bar.
Who's name they have forgotten.

Tumble

What is it?
This thing before you,
unknown and under examined.
What can you do to figure out
these questions, when question
continue to come. Every day brings
new conundrums twisting perfectly
into nostalgia.

When working men dream
of writing and writers dream
about fighting. Business people
wish to become ballerinas,
a crossing guard, a soldier. The question
of what he is in flux, a constant state
of tumble, with no grasp of place to
confuse life further.

Rock

Everyone
wants to be
a rock star,
but when you
actually meet one
they just want
to be quiet.
It's just a
matter of
prospective
and experience
or an industry
that sees
fit to steal,
cheat and
lie, in order
to extract
money from
hormonally
randy
teenagers.

star

I am still
the angry
teenager,
trying to
make sense
of a world I
just don't
see.
With every
day that
passes I'm
more
convinced
that I
will never
understand
the erosion
of time.
Or how
it will
eventually
kill me.

The Pole

At least pole dancers
are honest about selling their time
and bodies.

You do it for far less-money and sex.

You dance your merry parade,
peacock your wears whilst suckling at the
power teat.

Play clown for those owning more than you.

So the next time your boss asks you for your
time, remember to turn your head and ask
"do you like"

Not forgetting to wipe your chin and smile.

Forced...

Even more drunk now,
if you're not having fun
then what is the point?

Even if that fun comes at
the expense of sanity and
meaningful things.

Even if that fun stops
you working and doing
things you love.

Even if the fun takes over
your life and leaves you
with liver cancer.

Even if that fun replaces truth
with simpler versions then
replaces that with lies.

Even if you wake on someone
else's floor next to some person
you've never met.

Even though you know you're
not you when in it's
tangled clutches.

Even if you know you can be
so much more, in so many
other ways.

Even now you're looking for
another drink to erase the
memories of last night.

Even when there's no one
to hold you, because you stink
when you are that way.

Even though time is gone and
will never return in the
exact same way.

Even you know it has to stop
and you are the only one
to stop it.

Even out my friend...even out.

Notes on a music video
Melville - Televised

These days, so much importance and reality is based on unreal things. Characters from television programs have become real. So convincingly given life, by actors, that reality has become skewed.

Working in this industry I have a number of actor friends. On more than one occasion (Whilst out) I have witnessed fans approach and call them by a character's name...this is fascinating, a truly strange phenomenon.

When I first heard the Melville track Televised, I realized this would be the perfect opportunity to explore this topic. What would happen if these characters were, in fact, real.

In the video our heroine dies and then this 'fictional character' has her own journey towards whatever happens in the afterlife. I really wanted to show what this might look like. Moving down through the layers of life, from her childhood through her hopes, fears and desires.

This is why her styling changes so dramatically throughout the video. When she enters her fantasy world she changes to a vision of how she would like to look and act. A strong warrior, fighting against the confines of normality...an inspirational incarnation of self image. In this form she has no fear and is able to bring herself back from the brink of death and fight.

I really wanted the audience to go with her...believe that she is real, stand with her and fight. I knew that seeing her going against the system (whatever that might be) would inspire, but at the same time confuse. Almost a type of mob mentality, shouting and fighting but not really understand why you are doing either thing.

The end scene bringing a new level and twist on what they have just witnessed . The audience being brought back by a double reality check, then questioning what they have just seen and (Hopefully) wanting to watch it again.

That's one thing I aim for in all my music videos. A twist on what is real. I love to make videos that make people think and question, not just have a band backlit in a warehouse or large bottomed women bouncing next to a sports car. I find that extremely boring.

Give me a consciousness, within a fictional character, within an actresses imagination any day.

But, it's a lot to think about x

Robert Grant

Writer/Director

Dinosaur

I think every kitchen could be made
slightly warmer by a pink dinosaur mask,
hanging on a cork board.

Door frames covered in drawings of
unicorns and fairies. Photos from
family trips adorning every surface.

With a red wine in hand and hidden
cigarettes to be smoked after
bedtime books and laughter.

This house is the best place for
any man, especially a happy man
looking very much like me.

Jesus and the unicorn

"What's God?" my daughter asks me,
over cereal and apple juice.

"That's a good question" I reply,
slowly rotating my coffee cup.

"God is a way for many different people,
from many different places in the world
to understand how they came to be.
It gives them hope that there is something
more than just this world, and that there
is a reason for us to be here.
                              It's a story
so that we know how to live, what to do
and things that we really shouldn't do.
And when we make mistakes...fall over, that
there will always be someone there to pick
them up"

"Like you Papa" she says, arranging and
rearranging her sugar and milk, whilst
sipping juice like wine.

"Some, take comfort in never being
alone" my coffee cup now empty. "It's like a
story for confused and weak people to take
comfort in, make them feel better about
the world" I finish, receiving a swift kick to
the shin under the table from my wife,
hastily reddening with annoyance.

"People are fee to believe in what they
want to sweetie" Mrs. says, attached
hair stroke taking effect. "As long as what
they think doesn't hurt other people"
she adds, raising her eyebrows in unison.

"And what are unicorns?" the smaller asks,
as I sit back in my chair and my wife
mouths a firm 'NO!'
widening her eyes to scary.

See you, at six

You will never look upon
your daughter as a proud father.

That's impossible for you, but
it's all I will ever see.

Disturbed morning dreams, cuddled
away...surrounded by teddies.

Bashful lie admissions made truthful by
obvious situations.

Gymnastic attempts to copy ballerinas,
gracefully twisting hopes.

The beauty of a simply smile as I tickle your
belly with my beard.

You will see each situation differently to
me, for you are not me.

You are just you and cutely so, but age
will bring conflict.

                              So be ready my girl.

He

He is coming
I can feel him behind my eyes.

He is coming to make me see differently,
to strip my skin and show me a clock.

Make me nervously engage with
psychopaths…feel estranged from health.

He is coming to sodomize my body,
in my ears and eyes.

His dark fear engaging with glory and
hollow arguments.

With 'never again' speeches to this child
he once cared so deeply about.

He is coming
To breed with uncontrollable beauty.

                    …then he came by night.
                    …and upon the morning.

He left

I feel weak.
My body, no more
than sack of skin
holding these cold
bones in place.
Every movement,
cracking, grinding
questioning why.
He has used me to
out his vapid lusts.
Left me crumpled,
torn and folded
into this bed.
Smiling his toothless
grin so perfectly.
As he raises my chin
for the knockout.
Left here cold,
bleeding internally.

Japanese backside.

I just saw a post
about a women who is
a millionaire.

Every day she
takes a photo of her bum
and posts with a smile.

If it's that easy
to become a rich human
in this, our culture.

I would still want to
do something just slightly more
imaginative.

Although I am sure
there's a wide market for my
fantastical ass.

It's a question of Marriage

After ten, odd years, of marriage,
the only advise i can give to
a new husband is never...ever,
answer your wife
before she's finished
asking her question.

Even if every single syllable
in the very fabric of her
conversational structure
is leading down a familiar
circumstance towards a
known conclusion.

Even if you've judged her mood,
time of the day, week, month.
Rounded up for work situation
and general relationship status.
Considered your last impressions
of previous encounters.

Even then, after all that instantaneous
thought and contemplation.
Even if they have already asked
a similar question only minutes ago.
Always let your partner finish their chain
of thought or its the shit house for you.

And after these 10 odd years I can now
see why. For no matter who your partner
is, sex, color, species. Every single thing on
this planet needs respect. Needs someone
to care enough to let them finish
that thought, as you would ask of them.

Swollen genetics

My daughter (again) sits watching me work.

"What are you doing daddy?"

"I'm writing baby"

"Why?"

"Good question" my answer stops me mid flow.

"Do you want to draw horses with me?" she asks.

"Ok Baby"

"I'm pink and you're blue daddy...ok?" she says with a smile.

"Why?" I ask, moving round towards her.

"Good question baby" she answers as I swell with perception.

Non Tao A-ha

I'm watching old music videos in the office
through earphones, when my daughter
sneaks up beside me, unseen...
almost educing paralyses.

"What you watching daddy?" she asks
as I clamp my chest, breathing
dramatic and heavy. Then proceeding
to show her the world of Steve Barron.

"What is that?" she continues,
swinging on my office chair as I
move to the window, turn and answer...
"Imagination sweetie, pure imagination"

Answers

"You is a better man than me
in every way bar two...two" I say
throwing back another shot.

"Humility?" he's asks
nodding as if I'm making sense,
wincing after drinking the last mistake.

"Spoetry and booze" I slur, ordering
two more and winking like a twelfth round
boxer, badly losing his comeback fight.

"I'm not sure how important either
of those things are really" he's adds, as I
one hand steady myself against the bar.

"Twos things..." I slur through repartition.
Wondered now as I sit and write, to
how much of this is true.

"You're never going to remember this
conversation" he's adds, leading me to the
conclusion that he's probably wrong.

As I tap out these few words, in order
to tell you a small piece of nothing, only
comeback being…forth wall break.

The end of this story is inconsequential.
Irrelevantly sitting in the corner of my
office, wagging its little finger at me.

As the builders outside my office continue,
smashing hammers and pouring the
concrete, that will soon black out my sun.

So thinking back to that night, with that guy
in the bar. I'm not concerned by
by repeating, or repeating. Or…

Not worried about what was said or done.
Just concerned that my life is a fabrication,
a beautiful lie to hide behind.

The truth, being memories of childish
times, dreaming of doing exactly what I am
now doing on this day in that summer.

Of Monday morning monologues, after
Thursday night digressions, as even this
poem starts to sound already written.

In this past made purely of lies. When
this forth wall finally breaks and a far
fairer man will here sit.

Apologising to his readers of all those
tall tales, when small truths would have
perfectly sufficed.

The only thing I can now remember him
saying being, "Not everyone wants to talk
about poetry mate"

As I steady myself in his anger and ask what
he'd like to discuss. His answer coming back
as 'Science'…I settle in.

Not seeing the distinction now, between
what is real and what I want as fact,
or false or wrong.

If fact and truth, come from a memory of a
night that only happened because I willed it

and if, then maybe so.

No longer needing to use, interesting
writing technique at the beginnings of
poems, only to drop them by middle.

As these stories now require more lies to
keep up with old. So I should go and get
some passport photos, on my way out.

                    ...strange that...

@GeorgiewithaG.

It's hard to imagine that George Orwell
would even be famous these days.
If, the generation he predicted
existed in *his* time of being.

For to be known these days
it takes more than just talent.
I can't comprehend which selfies
he would put up on Instagram.

What social media posts would
be flagged up as suppressive content.
As these already bawled out faces
stare at other versions of this.

Creating themselves the same in
black lip stick or anarchy badges,
bought at a corporate skate shops
on the high street, next to Ikea.

Same, branded, skinny T'd jocks
turned to moving adverts by

lifestyle experts, consulting
on high day rates with perfect teeth.

Smile, snap, adjust, filter, publish. But
you're really being published are you?
Just giving more of the commodity up,
that being us, we and you.

TV celebrities giving advice to children
about anxiety and stress, because
their hair didn't fall quite right
in the mirror you bought them.

Forgetting that 'persona' means mask,
yet subconsciously adopting the notion.
As it seems as valid as any other
you heard this morning on the train.

Rattling towards a job you hate
and knees you will soon not have.
Thinking you did it different, when
you did it exactly the fucking same.

If I do

…damn you
oh you, the damned.
Drowning in wishes,
on death beds
you didn't earn.

What will this world
have me do, but
try and acquire the
end that comes
so easily to most.

Leaving something
here to signify that
even I existed
somewhere along
this vibration.

With a terrible want
to be made immortal
in these scratched pages
I worked so
damn hard for.

So damn you,
oh you, the damned.
With light fingers I'll type,
pained days feel, as
I sit on grassy banks.

Your appointed throne,
crumbles as memories
are made and forgotten.
To be excused in this life
you feel you lived.

Awaking my almighty,
with a load clap
announcing that
he is finally dead.

Oh you, the damned.

he is dead.

Time for a little chaos

Forget about time.
For time as you know it
is the only truly man made
thing on our planet.

It wasn't here before
we existed, like every
other element now combined
to make other things.

It wasn't present at
the formation of rocks
or the first creatures
sucking in air.

These things that needed
counting, in which ever
decimal or system it may be,
were already here.

Time came later,
bringing order and restraint.

Meeting times and
modernisation.

Timetables and schedules,
so physicists can theoretically
argue that it's been here
since the universe went boom.

When, In actual reality
there is only disorder
verging on chaos,
time a mere fabrication.

So be free to wonder
what to do with your time
knowing what you now do
...and act accordingly.

Dancers

Dignity is mine to give away as I see fit.
Although you may think me ridiculous
as I dance here on this plain wooden
table. You can't even begin to fathom
how superficial you seem to me.

Your dignity is hidden behind your
ego. Tucked back, lurking beneath...
eventually awakening in stroke or bad
parenting for everyone to see, as you
squirm in guttural intentions.

So let me just dance here for a second,
consider your dark half fully. For tomorrow
I will hang my head. So spent, to even think,
let alone to contemplate what an idiot I
was and how time is more important.

I fear you will never have those
experiences, wouldn't tolerate it in
yourself as you will not now, in me. You
judge yourself so harshly as to instill false
virtue, rather than just dance or sing.

May want to live a quiet life and
that's fine with me. Just don't judge me
too closely, for right now it's the dancer
you only see. Proceeding without your
acknowledgment, in times just to be.

All those words that you haven't said and
acting upon, sit dormant at feet so clean.
Let me dance...you fool, let me dance and
scream. For this is how I see you,
the way you now see me.

Dog fight

I see a woman
trying to wrestle a glove
out the mouth of
a dog named 'Bastardo'

For a second I consider
the beautiful irony,
until realizing it's simply
that she's Spanish.

Tomorrow, different

The 5am staggered bird call,
lit pink promises of foolish endeavor.
Of never doing what I have exactly
done…again, amidst many reasons to
consider myself heroic or wise.

The awaiting pin drop tip toe,
through a house I seldom comprehend.
Trying quiet, to retard my tiger tailed
anticipation of this morning breakfast, I
must curtail for fear of collapse.

My best, awoke three days from,
after time spent devouring worth -n- sugar.
Condemning ones vapid id, splitting will
dead center with order only to regain the
strength to do it all again…tomorrow.

More-ductive

out,
on some street corner
blurring into,
hiding from,
trying to make sense..
.trying to write,
conformed to cliché
no over used expressions
no passionate look ups
no convincers,
not to many no's
more rhythm
less blues,
more musically sound
more disguised wisdom,
less use of the word more
less cigarettes
more exercise
more listening to Radio Head
more days without the media social
less anxiety about real face time
or on stage,
in person...next to you.

Out of control
out of time
and rants about what?
about this
about that,
more time
more effort
more oral
less TV and sleep,
more crisp,
in this time.
more,
of
what
I
want.

Dark

Can't say why,
it just must.

Can't say how,
it just will.

Don't know when,
it just does.

Can't *run-hide*,
from its touch.

Can't bribe out,
far too much.

On that day,
I'll be ready my love.

Not wondering if baby…
just gone.

One last dance,
ending this song.

Coffee house Beats

She sits daydreaming
just as I, pondering words
uncomfortably sat
listening to bad Jazz music.

Gestures to mouth,
she looks quite intense.
Cascading hair, as
her mind unfolds.

Interrupted by telephone
I bashfully wonder
if I really know, this
woman at all.

Twirled pen amidst fingers
mimicking writers with
intensity like a manager,
sex queen, god.

Long hair hiding face
as beard does mine

consider whether I should
meaningfully give her this poem.

Romantic notions evaporating
with change of song, dryness
of coffee mouth, rendering
forced Jazz annoying.

The 13:31 from somewhere

He used to be different,
used to be something
that in his eyes was better.
Strong back, ladies swoon
then shake in his presence.

Now broken, he sits in
the restaurant, trying to
remember the glory days
back when he was shinny
and newly formed.

Now, the party years are matched,
caught up and crippled. Those
beers weigh heaving on nights
that no longer seem so important,
no meaningful introspective sky.

His conclusions now drawn from
failure, surface corrupted, smile
broken only asking for one more chance

to shine and impress the unimpressed,
who've seen it all before.

He laughs loudly, shakes his straw hair.
Runs hands over tattered beard
whilst asking the waitress for another.
Receives it, takes it down in one fluid
movement, not even waiting for cheers.

"Another!" he screams slamming the glass
down on the table, eyes turning from blue
to grey with every teary sip, as machismo
languishes in emptied challis, resting by
numbed arm and yellowing skin.

As the clock clicks to 13:32 on a Tuesday
afternoon, his demeanor shifts to that of
vulgar...gestures follow in suit, as does
whiskey and cider as the end is no longer
an option, in this here place, in only all time.

"Drink through" he screams, followed by
"Eating is cheating" follow tequila, follow
vomit, follow floor. Raising head only
slightly "Let's eat Schnitzel!" he screams
replacing head in vomit, then passes out.

About Bob

…come on now Bob!
It's time to buck those
ideas up and start this
year off well. Time for
something new for you-
-ve done this before.
It's time to live up to lies told.
In this place that you imagine
you once knew well.

…Now Bob came on!

Sorted and took steps towards.
Turned ideas into art after
realizing that it's always
time for something new.
This place that's so imagined,
is better off a mystery. To be
puzzled over until the day
you close those wide eyes.

bottle of piss

The day after I removed a bottle of stale
urine from the corner of my office I felt
better about myself as a human being.
More complete in some way.

As if last week's regret parade had
somehow elapsed. The toilet pushed away,
this now, brown congealed syrup,
my mind could finally return.

Understanding that those nights that lead
to a bottle of piss, are the things I tend to
write most about. The bottle itself, a
beautiful metaphor.

The last few days of recovery have given me
time and space to dissect self to distraction
and consider my life through the eyes of
an addict.

That wrinkled lemonade bottle has become
the condensation of regret dripping down

to my delusions of grandeur, as gods are
muzzled.

On flush, I turn to rub hands on trousers.
Particles entering the very fabric I exist
within, the very core of this woven universe
warming my pillars.

As I look up to see my reflection and realise
that maybe I'm thinking about this a little
too much or at very least exchanging
reality with some other form of neurosis.

For at least I didn't piss all over the floor.
Like back in those university drunk day
conversations in campus bars,
when study seamed irrelevant.

Not waking up on morning after vomit
stains down the bed frame, random
women next to me looking
more confused than I.

At least I made it home this time and
was organised enough to get a bottle and

fill it, undoubtedly getting some on
the floor, but that's a given.

Maybe everything is (in fact) going
to be alright and the world will
shift back to something I remember
to be the real.

This bottle of piss now a symbol
or hope and nuance and freedom,
amidst a world of corrupt giants with
anvils for hand.

We will survive...prevail at time when
all seams lost to tragic retold childhood
admitting plans to keep us all
apart and quiet.

All hail piss...all hail the imagination
of piss, the exact excretion of the past
to be flushed away and forgotten again,
after previous iterations.

It's all a bit dramatic really. For
some people may think me a nihilist

because life's simply bathos in physical
form...with piss stains on its trousers,

        bemused look upon its cherry face.

Fuck you right back

This old battle scared body
sits. Crumpled into a ball,
waiting to be burnt -n- bottled,
tossed away like everything
we don't see or care to.
Too many things now to get
checked, too many things
left to rot or grow fungus.
Finger skin creeping back
to scare itself into wanting
to start all over again. Hair
growing from unusual parts
and falling from the familiar.
Swallows sound tracked, back
clicked and crunched. Knees
swell red and bruised, wrists
as rusted barn doors on windy
days. Eyes arrested by the
foreground and confused before
the future. I wonder how long
it will be before I need medical
underwear and expensively ugly
off brown shoes. Wearing

clothes for comfort amidst
reason to watch rather than
play. Two showers and toilet
assistance required, with arthritic
memories of forgotten pasts
in that life I'm not sure I lived.

Late...home.

The end of this night brings
a disco in my head.

Looping pop music,
attended by people I despise.

In tales already told
on nights I've said I saw.

Staring at a ceiling
dancing me away from here.

Back to a point
before it ever happened.

On mornings when
nothing new will be made.

I'm left to consider
how better to have spent my time.

Brush

My daughter is in
the bathroom,
calling her hairbrush
as if it's a small dog.

I'm standing in
the kitchen,
wondering if red wine
can be called thusly?

3 Haiku

Pest

A six nipple beast,
stands over me snarling smoke
from every pore.

Youth

Back, when I was new
dreams came easily enough
to be forgotten.

Form

Life *IS* the visions
of some, who were never full
or even observed.

Old lady

She is a strange old bird
but she is my mum not yours.

Got me into Michael Jackson
and Frankie goes to Hollywood.
Sat me down and made me
experience Hendrix.

"Listen to that" she screamed and danced
and sung…with passion in her arms.

With these eyes she grew, I see Her.
The cranky old bird, screaming at un-boiled
pots, on stoves with no gas, in a house with
no warmth, she made me smile.

Always was a real odd duck, with wings
clipped, she can now only waddle.

Vertically kicking annoying black cats
wrapping circles around her legs,
whilst cooking meat and
two veg for evening dinner.

Is she alright?' No I'm half left"
her answer always brought a chuckle.

When I told her that I'd found the woman
for me, she paid for my travel,
even though she knew that woman
would take me away from her.

But she's my mum, keep your
hands off...get one of your bloody own.

For, even if she can't really walk now.
There once stood a different beauty...I've
seen the pictures of this hay day creature,
enchanting men in uniforms.

She's my mum god damn it, there's not
enough of her to go around.

May not have had confidence of her father,
travelled as much as my father, never
understood the philosophies
of this here son...poet

but that wonderful lump, my wonderful
Mum...has gold in her soul.

Cranes

I have hope that
we live in a world
where industrial cranes
are painted yellow
not for safety reasons,
but because they look beautiful
littering clear blue summer skies.

Mama

…and as harsh reality hits,
she saw a real world
more fully than before.

Her understanding grew,
for mummy was exactly right
…that knife really was sharp.

Brian

I just found out that an actor
who I admire greatly, died.
Years I watched him be the angry
policeman, I so wanted to be.

The smoothest tough cowboy you
have ever or *will* ever see.
Played in the cruelest film I ever saw, as
the most bigoted sheriff I've ever known.

That film about the guy coming back
from war, losing his mind and killing. Then,
a private eye, another cowboy, an actor, a
hero to his family and friends.

He loved what he did, with the heart that
gave out, but boy did he love his art.
Sleep well sweat prince and thanks for
making me feel cool, for half a second

x

Now...lady

I want to prove you right.
After all these years and excuses
I want to prove that your
dad was correct.
He saw it, but didn't say.
Your mother knows it,
but is in her own way.
You think of me what exactly
I am, that being...a bum.
But I'm your bum, our daughters
bum and father, a good one at that.
I may drink too much, from time
to tonight. May say too much
from always until now, but
I made you think... didn't I?
Just for a second I tilted
your head and you saw
this nonsense differently.
For we both know my gift,
as we both know yours,
whilst we tumble toward

infinity, holding trust as truth.
Hand in foot, against this world
that I help you misunderstand.

3 for 1

If I'm not going to drink
then I have to write,
for you don't want me
to be the man I am when
neither is getting done.

Falling over into that
man I don't like. The one
with no imagination
no spark into no
extraordinary life.

His biggest fear is one day
dyeing, emptying a dishwasher
or hanging up socks, instead of
one of life's pleasures.
Heart attack from on high.

So choose him, him or me.
then get comfortable
with your bastard choice.
For I'm staying here
to do something strange.

Warm inside, cold out.

Stand, see the world finally,
understand the point is
that you never truly will.

Then gaze down upon yourself,
and realise fully that you're...
wearing only socks.

As the builders
across from your office
return from laughter to work.

Your coffee break erupts
as your socks fall off
mid conversation.

You're left naked amidst
this stupid place that deems
it so unnatural.

Before the interview

"I want to be considered
          a more facile human"

                    she said, whilst tickling
her golden blonde hair
with an elaborately carved
blood red chop stick.

"I'm not sure you know exactly
                          what that means"

                    I replied, removing
my microphone...proceeding
to hum the Jaws movie theme
whilst widening my eyes.

"What the hell are you doing?
                    You're trouble"

          her retort coming with
a sharp jolt back
          into her white fluffy
                    mock 1970's hipster chair.

"Troubled...maybe"

I replied, just to break
no tension that hasn't really built.

In a conversation
that will never really matter.

Jim

I just sat and saw
an English/American
late night chat show host
eat a cockroach
marinated in clam juice,
on prime time T.V.

As I write this,
I'm still unsure
if I'm more horrified
that it exists or that
I just watched it, or that
44 million others also did.

Wondering what hope
I hold onto for humanity,
or future history,
If this is what passes for
popular entertainment,
in our broken culture.

Tangled

"Why can't I just be?
Realize my normality…with in
these confines of a confined mind.
Will some nuance, come to fruition"
I think, to myself…one morning whilst
trying to write an original something.
Seeing the horror in what I've just
written, then trying to use it in
a new, interesting way. Whilst
turning tables and writing…
about a process that I am
actually, now mocking
entangled wisdom,
questioned trust.
The experiment
here ends…
abruptly
as fuck.

Life staged

(Him)
"All the things I've done in life have brought
me to this point and I don't like it here"

(Her)
"So what are you going to do about it?"
(she asks, pouting from behind a coffee cup)

(Our *hero* raises his head and looks at her)

(Him)
"fantasize"
(he adds…dramatically)

Here lies James Watson

Will he become the man
he knows himself to be?
Does that man even exist
anymore. For the man
he used to know already exists.
He's exactly where he wanted to be
when last considering this very
same question, two books back.

So if you think about it, doubts
to his character are pointless.
The fact that he considered them
are as pointless as him thinking about
them in this present. He's badly
presenting, so to consider
if he will (Yet again) live up to
the standards that he holds for himself
are irrelevant, for he can only stand
up to his personal morality.

To even consider that he wouldn't,
negates the original question for he will
adapt his standards as he goes through his
life, in order to rectify current
circumstances, adjusting reason. As this
now, exorcises time and we are left with
emulating combinations of words and ideas
from a past of drop kick bars at 3:30 am
after saying for two hours that we must go,
before vices turn to tumours in our neck.

Vision blurred by desire, track across
eyes left weighted and annoying. For
that mans desires are already dead,
what is this place I now find myself?
Struggling with mortality in illusions of
lust, still thinking he'll be called out as
a fraud whilst talking in third person
to no one that's listening at all. Trying
terribly to finish this self indulgence
with a twisted smile on a tangled face.

That dirty old beast

"Come here"
he said,
arching a
talon hand
at me.
"Explore my
labyrinth.
Come in
get warm,
the next five hours
you're mine,
so get comfortably
in this, long hall"
he burns
tomorrow mornings
first light
into eyes
that don't
want
to see it,
don't even
want
to know

it exists.
"I'll make you
popular
amongst
strangers"
he adds
"make you
ask questions
and hear
answers you
don't care about
for that
is what
I do
to the mortal,
my gift.
Make you want
to taste her,
taste the sweet
dripping
down their backs.
Run your senses
red with lust
then take away
what you know
makes you

feel sexy.
Then
just when
you think
I'm getting out...
away from your
system,
I'll make you
want me
even more
for in there
lays my talent.
My aged eyes
will forever look
upon this world
and entice you to
ask for more.
I am you...
a better you,
cleaner
and more
presentable,
sweatier, yet you
will smell like
the man
you know yourself

to be,
in a world that's
yours for the taking.
So come
look round
my lair,
there's treasure inside.
For if this is not reality,
then let me show you
what it can be'

Slowly...Clear

We're waiting for the magnificent now
to present itself as surprise.
See everything for the first time, as if
it's easy to be innocent.

Wanting so much to understand our lives,
yet wonder what happens next.
This flux making us nothing...if not flexible,
infusing facts with wishes so beautifully.

On this merry vibration we sit, tumbling
through...never stopping to consider.
With no past accurately remembered,
within scenarios we've only dreamt.

She only sees him

"You got me reading my own shit"
I write in an 11:37 pm text message to a
woman that seems interested in my lilt.

"Well that's ok" she replays. "I got your
book in the post today"

"At this point, after this much wine...it's like
I'm talking to himself, about myself, inside
my own head, about something I can't quite
remember"

"I'm really looking forward to reading it" she
continues.

"Sometimes it feels as if the world has
ripped me out of a magazine and stuck me
to a collage, made up of memories that are
not really mine"

"I love the cover" I didn't reply anymore.
Just sit back at my desk, finished that damn

red wine bottle to wake up feeling like shit,
about more things than I was before.

Here she came

In those days, I had
to find more time.
For she took up
most of it, with
crying and shitting
in her tiny pants...
Disturbing thought
with cute joyful laughs.

I could only think
of her. Had to force
my last book out
in order to feel
a little relevant
within my own life.
As she now runs around
in the courtyard, giggling.

My contentment
realises her importance,
whilst allowing my
memory to describe
me a poet once more.

On this beautiful day
spent hearing kids
whoop and wail.

Her and friends doing
all the things we told
them not to do,
at times that should
be spent eating dinner.
Just as we did
when we where wild
and young and free.

I hear them laughing,
high pitch screaming
from the echoes
behind trees, that can't
be seen from far balconies.
In flowered sun hats
they run and prance
as horses and pixies.

…in the distance they are so happy,
which makes efforts, worth my time.

3 Thoughts

1.
Brown spot

Grass was always green,
I have just been staring at
bald patches to long.

2.
Bugged

I fear the brown bug
crawling up my office wall
understands how to live life
way more than I ever will.

3.
Smoke

She's amazed just how wide
I can dream, just how far I can see,
in directions her head has never turned.
For I am the smoke she grasps at.

brave man

He's courageous. If stood knee deep
in freezing mud, shit and guts,
spilled by broken promises...the
lied to masses after bonds made.

He would be the first to run towards an
unknown outcome...a screaming banshee.
Brandishing his father's crest...Celtic sword,
defiant in correction of unjustified actions.

He is love and honour, trust and valour
and fuck you who takes from him.
You are soft without men like these,
a weak country with tattered morals.

His last breathe will be screamed in
defiance of everything you told him to be.
Plunging a wide sword into your neck,
whilst screaming rhythmic victory.

Maddening

I just wrote
so furiously
that I started
sweating.

Do you realise
how fast
and hard you
must write
to do that?

Quickly realising
that it's 34 degrees
in August
and I'm sitting
on the toilet
reading Bukowski.

Life is

I am a dream that once was,
in a time that never existed.
Amidst people I don't admire,
in a culture that alludes me so.

Watching computerised movies to
pass time, hearing songs of no importance.
Thinking that we are so damn special
waiting, for the ultimate distraction.

Waking to have sex with our ego,
sharing too many meaningless interludes.
Seeking veneration *whilst* lie admitting,
that we actually don't remember.

I am a dream that seemingly once was
and that dream was certainly good.
Now spoilt by what I see before me,
in the time after...it all seemed good.

Sunshine skating

"What are you doing Papi?" she asks
slowing...as skate boots hit grass.

"I'm writing sweet heart" I answer, her head
haloed by a mid-summers sun.

"Why?" her response making me question
myself, as she turns to move away.

"I'm rolling" she adds gliding off making her
hair flow simple as if part of the breeze.

I return to writing...as everything seems as
it should actually be.

Shaggy, old

He sits next to me.
Pats my head
like a wet dog on
a bleak morning.

Jumping in and
out of puddles so muddy
as to blacken his
pristine white beard.

Proceeds to wash
his hands of it,
teasing fetch
in the aftermath.

Lays blame at my feet.
Parades around me
as if I simply don't see
that he's a sociopath.

His warm breath, moistening
my neck. His careful calls marching

minds into line, vaporising sent
as he does so, calmly.

He is steadfast, rigid, ingrained.
For he forgets that I also
have will, an ideology for
myself on these most strange days.

As you rub your tiny head
with tired hands, for we know
the simplicity of the answer that
we are both now acknowledging.

So relax, feel my boot heel
at your neck. Taste the crack
as I wrench your intentions to snap
then flowing warmth to sleep.

All this time saying that you fully
see me, forgetting that I also fully
see you flail on the ground,
beneath a bloody boot heel.

I remain...blind

The answer to life is death.
Knowing the inevitable will come, should
give you the freedom to do whatever you
want, yet you still don't.

It's not a matter of behaviour or lifestyle.
Not of bright bells and whistles, swallowed
and thrown back up by that child you once
were.

Not the constant nature of all good things,
becoming guttural or sanitized whichever
form you see fit to observe. Tuning in to be
spun out, laid down...in the dirt.

Letting go of the circumstances
of this life you think you're living, will
ultimately lead you to seeing that in the end
of every dark moment...quality will out.

It will be heard and heard again, always
seen and read again. For all time, by all

people as long as they are able to
understand...that they're blind.

This humdrum place, so rested in banality,
will seek out those who want to find it.
Yet quality will come, it's all around you,
forever. It's in you...your very core.

Money can't change it, can't whisk it away,
nor success or children. Not sex or sweats.
Only by imagination can we see past the fog
to consider yourself, a more splendid thing.

Find the quality amongst the smiles and
dream yourself a more interesting beast.
Then run to where the beast lives and love
and dance until they tire of dreaming.

Taking that dream as truth, to create a
better vibration for us to sit upon
and under and within, for one day you will
never see anything of quality again.

I'll smile

If life be a joke and we're
merely the comedians
searching for punch-lines
in places that we never
even knew to be funny.

Then we must at least
be enjoying our spot light.
Laughter and joy ringing our
red ears dry. Eyes stream
with the improbability of truth.

Only problem being that
it's difficult to make yourself
laugh all the time. Those
that do rarely wear their
laughter, on the inside.

So let us not forget
to at least smile around
others, these pop projectors.
For times of solitude will out us
whilst doing what we truly love.

Once again we trudge

I fear this loneliness has
caught up with my sanity.
Tapping on the entrails of
guts I thought once resonated.

Defined by lusts full looks from
women that aren't looking
my way. Outside bars that I
simply don't enjoy anymore.

Pitifully hammering the exact same
sentiment over a strangled mind.
On these echoes from a time
I so hopefully stepped back from.

To now sit and type out this self
indulgent rambling rubbish.
With time only to consider myself
a much more important human.

She

The world won't save you…only you.
But I love you, because you're reading
this and for as long as I have half a mind
to write, then I will. Remember that there is
someone in this hateful place that thinks
something of you. We are now bound
together in a torrent of pointlessness,
seeing no time unfound into nothing that is
ever understood, whilst attempting to
pull ourselves into a place that
makes no sense. Just us holding hands
stroking each other so softly that only
we can understand, that tomorrow
might just be perfect. At least better
than a today, that never really started
amidst friends we don't really know,
trying to make something click in a
world with no thumbs. We are the
dark half and we are here to spill
drink and dance, stupidly loud.

Her

Time to be freed.
We are toasting
informally, as we
dance gratuitously
with borrowed dreams,
laid bare at feet
that have no
perception
of now and then.
At least honest
enough
to know us a liar
about our temptations.

Tongue

I paint the infected foam
on my tongue, two bottles red.
Then continue dictating,
to make you ugly inept humans
pay attention to fact.

You are him and she is you,
we are here together. You wouldn't
like anyone to tell you what to do
or who to love. So why would you
imprint that on others.

Old Man

An old man sits, writing about his life.
Recants stories about someone else.
That person was famous and successful,
had brio in every cell, but it wasn't him.

An old man sits, writing about his life.
Seeing his achievements slip into fiction.
For he never was and never will be,
that man that no one really believes.

This old man sits, writing about his life.
Confused by a world left to idiots to run.
He sees that maybe just maybe, it's time to
be truthful amidst a life of unforgiving tales.

? mark

What do you really think?

Is the most difficult question to answer
and the most misunderstood.

For when everything is stripped away.
Pulled from what we have been taught
or shown how to behave.

Social media and 24 hours news...*gone*.
Our history teacher silenced in that corner.
Friends boxed alongside health gurus,
sitcoms and wrath filled preachers.

Every pre-conception evaporated like
alcohol from skin, on that day we got
into it, about racial stereotypes some
sun-soaked pub Sunday. With that guy
you'd never met before or since.

Our parents brainwashed away along with
other family members, telling us how it was
in the good old days. Hopes and fantasies

realised amidst confirmations of mistrust.
Every story ever heard, retold in a voice
closely resembling our own inside speech.

Just us…propped up, rounded down, made
to consider the gaps between fact and
myth. Everything tossed up and rewashed,
as if time were soap, seeping down a
washboard, towards a rusty bucket.

We see ourselves, we'll forgive mistakes,
forever configuring to get back to the point
intimately known as true self. Stripping
wallpaper to reveal, just plain white walls.

With which we can finally paint our
masterpiece. A meaningful self portrait, for
the first and most personal of time.

You are the hidden feelings…gut reaction,
tingling in your teeth. So listen.

As I ask again…What do *you* really think?

Then and then to here

Back home from great Pasta, best Pizza.
Barberra Red bubbling in my belly.
Back from my Bologna.

From hearing passionate evening
arguments…to crane clatter on dog shit
encrusted streets.

From long arched walks amongst the
beautiful and fashionable…to angry builder
and pedestrian complaints.

Long ambling strolls replaced by sharp
goaled struts, back to this place called
home, *that* city.

Pickpockets offer trinket to beggars
claiming deafness. Of those authentic
Tratorias to mocked up versions.

On memories we now sit, eroded by
dwindling capacity, to remember
anything real.

Rotisserie, Pig

Multi-millionaires sit gushing over one another, as workers pour cement in the rain.

Governments complain about plastic consumption with hands wide open for contribution.

Investors turn entire families out of their homes, then shout about the down town homeless problem.

Fast food chains grow, pays less and less for meat, acting surprised when the quality dips to dangerous.

We all want it right now, exactly on time...must go faster, yet never stop to question working conditions.

Now drunk belligerent demons, we spend little time pouring over the remnants of that thing we once so valued.

Smashing special offer Vodka bottles
through shop windows because someone
we've never met, told us to.

Shame on the little piggy's that never stop
for a second to wonder if they should be
doing, rather than doing what they are.

You. Product of a middle point, that
evolution has handed you via history,
as your bib grows red with off cuts.

Now be quiet you reason to stop trying,
you abomination to what this race
could really do with comprehension.

Try, for one day. Not to turn on the spit.
Skin as leather, eyes burnt out,
mind on automatic rerun.

1988

At School, swinging legs under desks,
the beautiful popular kid slides in.
Sporting the latest trainers, telling stories of
how he met that player from that team.

Hair perfectly catching sunbeams,
reflecting them back on his bright blue eyes.
As I…swing local market bought, knock off
high tops, trying hard to emulate his stare.

"So what did you do this summer?" I ask,
waiting to be ignored. "I went to America
with my family" his reply coming at a time
in History, when that was still pretty rare.

"Me too" becoming the first of two lies I
would tell "Where did *you* go? (him)
"Miami, sat in the A-Team van" (me) the
second lie flows from fat kid in cheap shoes.

To this day I still remember saying them,

amidst thousands of lies I've now told.
Those two falsehoods, combining childish
popularity story, stand wide in jaded mind.

"You never sat in the A-team van Bobby"
said Lisa, a cute girl from my class.
"Did too...and I touched one of the guns"
I reply, confidently knowing my truth.

Later that morning Lisa gave me my first
ever kiss...based upon the lies told. Forever
cementing the reality of every relationship,
from that day until now.

        I saw the popular boy once more,
whilst visiting family. Ran into him at an old
pub, now converted to a convenience store,
just up the road from my Mums house.

He looked straight at me but, didn't recall.
His hair still thick in caramel gold, his eyes
just as blue. His trainers still brightly
glowing in the mid morning village sun.

He'll always be better looking, with a more winning smile than me, but there is one big difference. He never got to sit in the A-Team van...did he!

The Woodpecker paradox

Half way down a wooded lane,
away from my mother's house
I find myself hearing a woodpecker.

Stopping on a concrete bridge
over a man made brook,
I see a dark space before me.

Can't quite see the end nor know
if this is the beginning, yet wonder how
far this trembling mist stretches.

Getting closer...leaving the safety of that
bridge to explore this confusing place,
it salivates my advance .

On entering, I stumble through blind,
helplessly feeling the warm walls,
wet...comfortingly familiar.

After time of exploratory ambling,
light is finally presented before,
as if always existing.

I reach and pass through to find myself
on that same exact bridge on which I
started. Just older now, less energetic.

I look down at dirty feet, stiffening my spine
abruptly and continue down this wooded
lane, listening to an egg vibrating.

Meat

If this realism has finally shown itself to be
gracious, then I have become a man at last.
Younger versions of self, stand before this
once splendorous prison with
rusty hammers.

Of this past I speak so fluently and in
this time that seems so solidly formed.
I have decided to see it no more, for it
simply flows past me...as condensation
on soda can.

Now with wine to drink and diets to
change, I have become willingly older.
Ready to vacate, only of legacy do I think
and mutter under a breathe of rancid fruit,
behind walls of un-solid glory.

Childish

When you first become a parent,
you soon realise that everything
you thought you'd worry about
is nothing to worry about at all.

After seven (or so) years, it's the things
you never saw coming, that throw
you the most. Tip you off kilter,
tickle your dormant temper.

My daughter hates wearing socks.
Might sound trivial, verging on dumb
and I agree it's really...*really* silly. So why
won't she just put her fucking socks on?

A place that doesn't move

Just leave me under that tree my love,
near the place where you grew up.
So when you want to talk to me,
you'll know exactly where to look.

And every time you need to find,
you'll know exactly where I lay.
Just waiting here, as quietly can
holding hands to softly say.

We chuckled, we cried and often lied,
slamming doors in stupid fights.
No matter when you need to talk,
I'm here…on cold clear nights.

Here to bust clouds again, eat ice cream
again, on bright clear sunny days.
And when those skies are all shone out,
I'm here…in different ways.

Will try to explain the world I see,
in words on tickled ears.

And when you got scared of those tiny
things, you always faced your fears.

You always knew what you wanted to be,
were defiant when hungry or tired.
Screwing up your face or stamping a foot,
proclaiming as a dancer you'd be hired.

Know, the only real thing I ever did,
in this tangle I called my life.
Was to hear you laugh and watch you grow
in this house I made with my wife.

Watched you tumble down, howl and wail,
the day that skateboard died.
Believed, nodded and didn't discredit when
you answered "it was dragon, he lied".

So close your eyes, lay back, relax
and even stay a while.
Just put me under our tree little love,
I'll tickle sides when in need of a smile.

I'm waiting here to listen to you
and will always be your Dad.

Whose face grew wrinkled, grey and torn,
but mind was eager and glad.

Smile on these yellow fallen leaves,
cascading on the floor. You'll never
know just how much we loved
and how much we actually saw.

So put me under that tree my love,
just tuck me in nice-n-deep.
I'll wait until you need me back,
as I need you now I sleep.

In this chaos we drifted, spirit always lifted
I had you and you definitely got me.
My brave little one, be ever assured
he was happy that I became we.

So now bury me right here my love,
under that old and broken tree.
My little girl has up and grown,
fighting the world I helped you see.

my Ruby... Love Papa x

"We don't magically lose our ego. It's slowly and painfully kicked out of us over time."

Robert Grant 2022